Oswald Joseph Reichel

Solemn Mass At Rome In The Ninth Century

Oswald Joseph Reichel

Solemn Mass At Rome In The Ninth Century

ISBN/EAN: 9783744789035

Printed in Europe, USA, Canada, Australia, Japan

Cover: Foto ©ninafisch / pixelio.de

More available books at **www.hansebooks.com**

SOLEMN MASS AT ROME

IN THE

NINTH CENTURY.

BY

Rev. OSWALD J. REICHEL, B.C.L., M.A., F.S.A.

SECOND EDITION, WITH ADDITIONS.

REPRINTED FROM VOL. I., NEW SERIES, OF

Transactions of Exeter Diocesan Architectural and Archæological Society.

JOHN HODGES,

BEDFORD STREET, STRAND, LONDON,

1895.

May He Who has inspired so many faithful souls to pray for unity, in His own good time fulfil the prayer of their devotion, that instead of being derisively described as " a society of good men differing from one another in all their opinions but all earnestly seeking for the truth with the certainty that it never has been and never will be found," the whole Christian Body throughout the world may in verity and truth be united in Him ; " AS THOU FATHER ART IN ME AND I IN THEE, THAT THEY ALSO MAY BE ONE IN US ; THAT THE WORLD MAY BELIEVE THAT THOU HAST SENT ME " !

À la Ronde, near Lympstone,
6 *July*, 1895.

SOLEMN MASS AT ROME IN THE NINTH CENTURY.

Originally read at the College Hall, Easter, 1893.

———

THERE are two reasons for supposing that the subject of Solemn Mass at Rome in the ninth century is not alien from the objects of this Society. 1, Since the Council of Clovesho in A.D. 747 decreed (Can. 18) :

> That the holy festivals of our Lord's nativity in the flesh
> be uniformly observed, viz., in the office of baptism
> and the celebration of masses . . according to the
> written copy which we have from the Roman Church[1] ;

the Roman rite as used in the eighth century was by the canon law of this country the only authorised rite here then. 2, Since the earliest *Ordo Romanus*, of which we have a copy,[2] contains this direction : " Bishops presiding over cities do in all respects as the Pope does"; the Roman rite was by the rule of Rome sanctioned for use elsewhere. We may therefore say with certainty that the order for solemn mass at Rome at the beginning of the ninth century was also the order for solemn mass at Sherborne in the same century ; and that it was adopted as the order for solemn mass at Crediton when that town was constituted the centre of a Western See in the year 909 A.D., and likewise for Exeter when the See was transferred thither by Leofric in the year 1050 A.D. Hence the interest to us of Solemn Mass at Rome in the ninth century.

———

[1] Haddan and Stubbs, Ecclesiastical Documents, iii. 367. Batiffol Histoire du Bréviaire (Paris, 1894), p. 30, observes that in France, as 100 years previously in England, the Roman Liturgy was the result of personal initiative. The Holy See consented to it, but in no way provoked it.

[2] Muratori Liturgia, Venice 1748, i., 987.

I. Definitions and Introduction.

To begin by defining terms. Of old the word "mass" was used in the Gallican Church to describe any office which was concluded by the bishop by a *collectio* or summing-up prayer.[3] Thus the office after which catechumens were dismissed was called the catechumens' mass, the office of prayer of the faithful was called the mass of the faithful.[4] The Council of Agde[5] in the sixth century speaks of morning, mid-day, and evening masses to describe simple offices of praise and prayer held at these times, and directs the people to be dismissed at the end of each by the bishop with a summing-up prayer (*collecta oratio*). Ethelred's synod[6] of the year 1014 A.D. directs a mass or office of prayer to be said for the king at every morning mass. As the consecration of the Eucharist was the chief office of prayer, the term "mass" came in time to be exclusively reserved to that part of the service. Isidore of Seville about the year 630 A.D. writes : "Order of the mass, *i.e.*, of prayers by which the sacrifices made to God are consecrated."[7]

By solemn or, as it was formerly called, stational[8] mass, is understood the corporate and collegiate celebration of the Holy Mysteries in which the priesthood of the whole Christian family[9] is directly and not vicariously exercised, each one according to his position (*ordo*) in the Church contributing his share

[3] Walafrid Strabo, A.D. 849, in Migne cxiv. p. 920 ; Micrologus, A.D. 1070 in Migne, cli. p. 979. See Maskell's Ancient Liturgy of the Church of England (Oxford, 1882), p. 210.

[4] Augustin. Serm. 49 (al. 237): Fit missa catechumenis ; manebunt fideles. Avitus of Vienne, A.D. 500, Epist. 1 : In churches, palaces and courts (prætoriis) mass is said to be over (fieri pronunciatur) when the people are dismissed from attendance.

[5] Canon 30, in Gratian's Decretum, Pars iii. Distinctio V. caput 13.

[6] Can. 5.

[7] De Officiis, c. 15.

[8] Duchêsne Origines du Culte Chrétien, p. 153.

[9] 1 Pet. ii. 9 ; Rev. i. 6 ; Duchêsne, p. 171.

thereto.[10] " Let each one," says St. Clement,[11] " take part in the thanksgiving service (εὐχαριστείτω) according to his own order." In non-solemn mass the priesthood of the laity and the deacon is exercised vicariously by the presbyter together with his own,[12] either without the assistance of anyone save a collet or parish clerk, or with the aid of a titular deacon and sub-deacon as in a quasi-solemn or high mass. Although solemn mass has now become obsolete, even at Rome itself since 1870, yet for well-nigh twelve centuries until the up-growth of the parochial system it was the only service of obligation for all Christians. Private masses were tolerated rather than approved services in the ninth century,[13] and as late as the fourteenth were not allowed to draw off persons from attendance at the public and quasi-solemn service which then did duty for it.[14] A review of solemn mass as it was originally celebrated will therefore be helpful in explaining the

[10] Bona Rerum Liturgicarum Lib. i. c. 13, Trèves, 1747 : Solemn mass, now called conventual, canonical, capitular, principal, or greater, is one conducted with music and the solemn apparatus of ceremonies, ministers and assistants to the clergy, each exercising the functions of his order, together with, in ancient times, the whole body of the people offering and communicating.

[11] 1 Ep. ad Corinth, c. 41.

[12] Walafrid Strabo De rebus ecclesiasticis, c. 22 : Although when a priest offers alone, those for whom he offers are co-operators in the same consecration (actio) whom the priest also represents in certain answers, yet it is not a lawful mass unless a priest, a responder, an offerer, and a communicant are there. Le Brun (ed. 1777), iv. 5.

[13] Gallican canon in Gratian iii. Dist. i. c. 52 ; Theodulf Cap. 7, A.D 787 : A mass-priest ought by no means to sing mass alone without other men, that he may know whom he greets. . . He ought to greet the bystanders, and they to make the responses. Cap. 45 : We command all mass-priests who are willing to sing mass before high mass that they do it secretly, so as to draw no part of the people from high mass. For it is an evil custom which some men practice to hear mass early in the morning, and then presently afterwards serve their own belly. . . We command that no man taste any meat till the service of the high mass be finished.

[14] Const. 5 Winchelsea, A.D. 1305 : Let not stipendiary or any other priests . . receive any oblations. . . Let the said priests on Lord's days, or when a dead body is there present, begin their masses after the Gospel at high mass is ended.

origin of private masses and also certain other peculiarities of mediæval practice, which at first sight seem anomalous.

The earliest extant account of the Eucharistic service at Rome is that given by Justin Martyr in his first Apology, c. 67 :

> " On the day called Sunday (he says) all who live in cities or in the country gather together to one place, and the reminiscences of the apostles or the writings of the prophets are read as long as time permits. When the reader has ceased, the president verbally instructs and exhorts to the imitation of good things. Then we all rise together and pray. . . When prayer is ended, bread and a mixture of wine and water are brought in to the president, who in like manner offers prayers and thanks-givings according to his ability, and the people assent, saying Amen. And there is a distribution to each and a participation in that over which thanks have been given. And to those who are absent a portion is sent by the deacons."

According to this account, which represents the Roman rite about the year 140 A.D., the service appears then to have consisted of four parts, viz., (1) public readings followed by the president's instruction or sermon, (2) prayers made by all the people, (3) the long prayer of the president after the bringing in of the already prepared bread and wine, and (4) the communion of those present and the conveyance of the hallowed Elements to the absent. Taking these four points as landmarks, let us endeavour to see what form they assumed in the solemn mass of the ninth century, using as authorities the two Ordines published by Muratori, and more particularly the Ordo lately published by M. Duchêsne from the MS. of St. Amand,[15] which M. Delisle contends belonged formerly to Gautier, Bishop of Orleans, and descended from him in A.D. 895 to his nephew Gautier, Archbishop of Sens.[16]

---

[15] In Duchêsne Origines, &c., p. 440, from Codex Parisinus, 974.
[16] Sur d'anciennes Sacramentaires, p. 115.

II. The Readings.

The first point which deserves attention is that the service originally began with long readings. It is well known that in the East, in the fourth century, there was a preliminary service, consisting chiefly of readings. The author of the Apostolical Constitutions (ii., 57), enumerates five sets of readings, taken respectively from the historical books, the prophets, the psalms, the epistles and gospels. These were conducted by the Λειτουργοὶ *i.e.*, the deacons and their assistants[17] and at all of these catechumens were allowed to be present. Hence this preliminary service was called the catechumens' mass.[18] In the Gallican Church the usage must have been similar, except that there were only three sets of readings ; the first from the Prophets, followed by a psalm afterwards known as the Gradual[19] ; the second from the epistles, followed by the *Benedicite* and *Alleluia ;* the third from the Gospels. The Gallican Council of Orange, A.D. 441, Can. 18, decreed that "the Gospels be read before catechumens in all churches of our provinces." In the Roman Church the practice was different. There the Gospels were regarded as belonging to the service of the faithful and in consequence the catechumens were excluded from being present whilst they were read until after the third scrutiny before baptism they had been initiated into the Creed and the Lord's Prayer.[20] The preliminary service there consisted of readings from the historical books and the prophets only, and ended

---

[17] Dionysius Areop. De Eccles., Hier. c. 3.

[18] Concil. Valent. A.D. 374, can. 1 : Ut evangelia ante munerum illationem in missa catechumenorum in ordine lectionum perlegantur. Ambros. Epist. 14 ad Marcell. : Post lectiones atque tractatum (the sermon) dimissis catechumenis.

[19] Raban Maur. A.D. 819, De Cler. Inst., I., 32 : That responsary is called the step-psalm (graduale) because it is chanted at the step (gradus) of the reading-desk (pulpitum). When a single person chanted the whole it was said to be rendered *tractim.* When it was chanted in alternate verses it was said to be rendered *antiphonally.*

[20] Amalarius De Eccl. Offic. iii. 36 : Our custom is to repel catechumens before the Gospel is read. Duchêsne, 287, 289,

with the entrance of the Bishop to say the summing-up prayer or collect for the catechumens.

III. THE PEOPLE'S PRAYERS.

The next point closely connected with a change which will be hereafter mentioned is the disappearance of the people's prayers, which in Justin's time were said aloud after the readings,[21] or rather the relegation of them to a separate service and the substitution in their place of the collect, called *super oblata* or *secreta*.[22] It is true this change was a gradual one and not fully completed in the ninth century. The saying of prayers aloud by the people had been then discontinued. The people were, however, still invited by the deacon to pray. A suitable pause was made while they prayed silently. At its close the Bishop said aloud the summing-up prayer. Previously, however, to the twelfth century the prayer called *super oblata* was the offering prayer of the priest himself, and was said by him in silence, as the rest of the people prayed in silence, the prayer of consecration with the Lord's prayer

---

[21] In the fourth century, the people's prayers concluded with prayers for catechumens, penitents, and the faithful themselves, each set of prayers ending with the bishops collect. It is probable that at Rome the public prayers for penitents were dropped in the time of Pope Leo (440-461), for one of his letters (Ep. 80 in Labbé iii. 1374) contains a direction that to prevent any being kept back from repentance through fear of having openly to confess their sins " it shall suffice if they make confession first to God and then also to the priest who approaches to pray for the sins of the penitent." At the time when Christianity was introduced into this country, public prayers for penitents appear not to have been in use ; for Archbishop Theodore in his Pœnitential (1, xiii. 4, in H. & S. iii. 187) says that " in this country there is no public reconciliation because there is no public penance." In the Gallican Church solemn discipline seems to have continued up to a later date, for the Council of Lyons, A.D. 517, can. 6, speaks of it as then existing. What is more, there is extant a letter from Innocent III. to the Bishop of Poitiers, A.D. 1199 (in Decret. Lib. 1 Tit. iv. c. 3) in which that Bishop is directed to discontinue the practice of awarding discipline solemnly by the vote of all.

[22] It is called Secreta in the Gelasian Sacramentary, Super oblata in the Gregorian. Walafrid Strabo, A.D. 849, says : " Anciently the offering and communion were done in silence." Micrologus, c. ii., in Migne, c. 41, p. 983 ; " The Roman order has no offertory prayer, the Gallican has."

being regarded as the summing-up prayer.[23]

IV.—ADDITIONS AND CHANGES.

Several important additions were made at the beginning of the service after the time of Justin. Some of these date back to the third century, others were made in the fifth century, when the Roman Church which had previously been puritanically conservative began to absorb foreign elements in its ritual, with more zeal than discretion.

(1.) The first change to be noted which is certainly as early as the third century is the separation of the preliminary service of prayer for catechumens, penitents, and the faithful, which was concluded by the bishop's collect, from the actual service of the Eucharistic Consecration. The people's prayers were conducted by themselves, or by the deacon, and appear to have been of considerable length constituting a παννυχίς or all-night service. After the decline of solemn penance they assumed the abbreviated form of a Litany, now known as the *Kyries.* As late as the ninth century the connection between the Kyries and Collect was understood at Rome, as appears from the fact that when the Litany was said in procession before a stational mass[24] it was followed immediately by the bishop's collect at the stational Church. Subsequently ritualists who failed to understand this connection expressed it by saying that, on procession-days the Kyries and Gloria in Excelsis were omitted. That the Litany must have been adopted in the Cisalpine Church in the sixth century is clear from the third canon of the Council of Vaison in 529 A.D.

(2) The second change closely connected with the preceding was that the first collect lost its original character as the close of the people's prayer before the great service commenced with the

[23] Duchêsne, 165, 192.
[24] Duchêsne, 156,

reading of the Gospels,[25] and came to be looked upon in a new light as the opening prayer of that service, the *oratio ad collectam* or prayer of meeting.

(3) Two other changes were also made which are further evidence of the altered view of the collect; one the introduction of an opening anthem called *Introit* at Rome, *Ingressa* at Milan *Officium* at Toledo and in the Sarum rite, the other the introduction of a hymn, the *Gloria in Excelsis Deo* at Rome, the *Trisagios* or *Aius*[26] in the Gallican rite which was inserted between the *Kyries* and the collect. Pope Celestine is credited with having introduced the Introit at Rome about the year 430 A.D. It consisted of a variable passage from the Psalms chanted by the choir during the entrance of the bishop in procession, as is still the use on Candlemas Day and Ash Wednesday in the Roman Church. At other times in accordance with the necessities of non-solemn masses it is said by the priest. St. Augustine mentions it as customary in Africa in his time,[27] and the author of the treatise which goes by the name of Dionysius the Areopagite also mentions it in the fifth century.[28] In the Byzantine rite a fixed and not a variable anthem

[25] An indirect proof that the great service originally began with the Gospels may be gathered from the place of ordination. This was required to take place (1) before the great service began, and (2) after the catechumens had been dismissed by the Council of Laodicea, A.D. 363, Can. 5. The custom has therefore been kept up of ordaining presbyters and deacons before the Gospel, although the Gospel is no longer the beginning of the service. On the other hand, the ordination of the Bishop of Rome, in strict conformity with the old rule, takes place before the beginning of the actual service, *i.e.* according to Innocent III. in Decretals Liber 1, Titulus vi., c. 28, before the Gloria in Excelsis.

[26] Aius = Ἅγιος viz. the hymn " Holy God, Holy Almighty, Holy Immortal, have mercy on us." This hymn is only used in the Roman service on Good Friday.

[27] Retractiones II. c. 11.

[28] De Ecclesiastica Hierarchia, c. 3 : He then (*i.e.*, after censing the enclosure of the sacred place) returns to the divine altar and begins the sacred chanting of the Psalm.

is used, the so-called Μονογενής, or anthem of the Only-t
The *Gloria in excelsis Deo* has been used as the hymn be.
collect at Rome from the time of Pope Symmachus, A.D. 50.
before the eleventh century it was only said by the bishop and
by presbyters except on Easter day.

(4) It should also be born in mind that at Rome in the fift.
century the instruction or sermon had been discontinued except on
special occasions[80] and that the custom of reciting the creed had
not as yet come into use.[81]   After the reading of the Gospels,
the book was handed to each one who devoutly kissed it saying
" I believe it " or " I confess it."

V.   The Offering.

According to Justin Martyr's account the prepared offering
was next brought to the president whose prayer over it was the
summing-up of the prayers which the people had been themselves
making.   As his account was written for the use of a heathen
emperor, we can well understand his omitting to give particulars
as to the manner of making and preparing the offering.   From
other sources we learn that the offering itself was threefold, corres-
ponding with three distinct positions in the Church held by (1)
laymen, (2) deacons (3) presbyters.   First was the offering of the
materials necessary to make up the outward representation of the
Lord's Body, viz. bread and wine, corn or flour and grapes.

[29] " O only begotten Son and Word of God, existing from everlasting,
Who didst deign for our salvation to take flesh from the holy Mother of
God, the ever-virgin Mary, and didst become really man and wast crucified,
Christ our God, Who by death didst trample upon death, One person of the
blessed Trinity, glorified with the Father and the Holy Ghost, save us."

[80] Sozomen, vii. 19.

[81] Augustin, Serm. 58, in Math. : The Lord's Prayer is said every day
in church at the altar, and the faithful hear it there, but you do not hear
daily the creed.   Sozom. i., 19, about A.D. 445, states that he was anxious
to give the creed of Nicaea, but several pious persons pointed out to him
that this kind of thing ought only to be in the hands of bishops and
presbyters.   The saying of the creed was instituted at Rome in the time
of Benedict VIII. A.D. 1012-1024. See Migne, cxlii. p. 1060.

These offerings were made by all the faithful.   Next was the corporate offering which consisted in selecting some of the materials offered by the people, mystically preparing them to represent the Body of Christ in union with His people and presenting them as such upon the Church's altar on earth,   This was the deacon's offering.   And lastly comes the heavenly offering made by the Great High Priest to His Father, whereby the earthly offering is hallowed.   As the heavenly offering is procured by the unanimous prayer of the whole body of the faithful[82] summed-up and presented to God by the presbyters, this was commonly spoken of as the presbyters' offering.

1.   Although there is no mention of the people's offerings in Justin's Apology, yet that such offerings were in use in his time is clear from the fact that they are mentioned in his dialogue with Trypho.[83]   They there bear the name of sacrifices, and both Irenæus and Tertullian in the second century use the same expression.   There seems good reason for believing that these sacrifices were made whenever practicable in grain or flour, and, at the proper season of the year, in grapes.   The Apostolic Canons, which represent the Eastern use in the fourth century, expressly mention (Can. 2) offerings of grain and grapes.   Moreover the words of the " Teaching of the Apostles " ix. 4 :

> As this broken bread was scattered upon the mountains and
> gathered together became one, so let Thy Church be
> gathered together from the ends of the world into Thy
> Kingdom ;

no less than Cyprian's words, Ep. 75 (Oxf. 69) 6 :

> When the Lord calls bread combined out of the union of
> many grains His Body, He indicates our people whom He
> bore as being united ; and when He calls the wine which
> is pressed from many grapes and clusters collected together

[82] Cyprian De Unitate Ecclesiae, c. 12,
[83] c. 28, 117.

His Blood, He also signifies our flock linked together by
the mingling of a united multitude

would lose much of their significance unless it had been the
custom then, as in some parts of Christendom it is still, to use for
the Eucharist bread and wine specially prepared out of the
combined offerings of the faithful to represent a united body. Such
a custom seems also to be implied by the language of Ignatius in
his letter to the Romans (c. 4) as quoted by Irenæus (Haer 28,
4) : I am the wheat of Christ and am ground by the wild beasts'
teeth, that I may become the bread of God." It is more clearly
expressed by Cyprian (Ep. 62, Oxf. 65, 13) : " In the sacramental
representation our people are shown to be made one, so that in
like manner as many grains collected and ground and kneaded
into one mass make one bread, so in Christ who is the heavenly
Bread we may know there is one Body."[84]   Walafrid Strabo
(c. 16) in the ninth century repeats the same.

As grain or flour must have been offered early in a long service
or it would have been impossible to bring it in to the president
already prepared as bread before its close, it would appear that
before the fifth century (when the services were abbreviated)
oblation-loaves called obleys, ubbles or hosts, already baked and
prepared, came to be offered by the people.   Pope Innocent in his
well-known letter to Decentius[35] A.D. 416, takes objection to the
Gallican practice of reading out the names of those who offered
before their oblation-loaves (hostiae) were presented to God by
the priest.   The fifth Council of Arles, A.D. 554 (Can. 1) requires
the loaves offered by the people to be all of one shape after the
pattern used in the Church of Arles.   The Council of Macon,
A.D. 585 (Can. 4) requires all, both men and women, to make an

---

[84] Augustine de Cio. Dei. x. 20 : The Church being the Body of Christ
learns to offer itself through Him.   *Ibid*, xxii. c. 10 : The sacrifice is the
Body of Christ, which is not offered to the martyrs, because these Body
the martyrs themselves are.   *Ibid*, x. 6, See Reichel's Manuals of Canon
Law.   The Eucharist, p. 87, note 45.

[35] Gratian, iii. Dist. i., c. 73.

offering of bread and wine every Sunday.   Archbishop Theodore[86] about 673 A.D. states that the Greeks allow both men and women to offer bread and wine, but that the Romans only allow men to offer.   Walafrid Strabo, A.D. 849 (c. 22) complains that "some offer inordinately, who, considering the number of oblations rather than the virtue of the sacraments, often offer cursorily at masses at which they decline to assist."   And in consequence Hincmar (c. 16, 2) A.D. 852 forbids anyone to offer more than one oblation-loaf for himself and his family, directing other gifts to be made before or after the service.   In Portugal wine only and not grapes must have been offered since the Council of Braga[87] in A.D. 675 forbad the use of freshly-made wine.   And the Trullan Council in A.D. 691 forbad generally the offering of grapes (Can. 28).   In this country the Council of Chelsea, A.D. 787, Can. 10, directed whole loaves to be offered and not detached pieces.[88]

As the offering of the Church is before all things required to be a pure offering,[80] which it cannot be unless those who present it and are as it were the constituent parts of it are themselves pure, it was the rule for the bishop to receive the oblation-loaves in person that he might know whose to receive and whose to

---

[80] II. vii. 4, in Haddan and Stubbs, iii. 196.

[87] Gratian, iii. Dist. ii. c. 2.

[88] Haddan and Stubbs, iii. 452.

[89] Διδαχη xiv. 1 :   On the Lord's Day come together and break bread ; and give thanks after confessing your transgressions that your sacrifice may be pure.   Irenaeus Haer. iv. 17, 5.   To emphasise this purity, Leo I. A.D. 440–461, is in the Liber Pontificalis said to have added to the canon in the prayer Supraquae the words "a holy sacrifice, an unspotted offering."   Walafrid Strabo, A.D. 849, De rebus eccles. c. 22, asks whether this means that Leo inserted these four words only, or whether he added to the canon all the words which follow.   Le Brun, II. 139, replies that he only added the four words, as is proved by the remark of Hilary in Quaestiones in Nov. Testament. No. 109.   Dionysius Areop. De Eccles. Hier. 3 : Those who are not altogether uniform and entirely without spot and blemish are excluded.

reject,[40] whilst the deacon in attendance received the oblation-wine. Those who by falling into sin had lost their priestly character were excluded from offering until their period of penance was over and they were restored to the Church. Nor was this rule relaxed even when, as in Archbishop Theodore's time,[41] penitents were allowed to communicate before their full period of penance had expired. Thus the Spanish Council of Lerida in 523 A.D. (Can. 13) forbids the offering to be received of one who allows his children to be baptized in heresy. Nicolaus I. in 864 A.D.[42] permits a matricide to communicate after doing penance for ten years, but forbids him to make an offering until the whole twelve years of penance are fulfilled. So late as the twelfth century, Eugenius III, in 1146 A.D., allows criminals about to be executed for some gross crime to receive communion, but forbids any offering to be made by them.[43] After the establishment of the parochial system and the constitutions of Archbishop Gray (Const. 2) in 1250 for the northern province, and of Archbishop Peckham in 1281 (Const. 27) for the southern province, which required every parish constituted a cure of souls to provide collectively the oblation-bread and wine, the people's offertory became obsolete in non-collegiate churches, and in collegiate churches the cure of which was committed to a vicar, it was usual to stipulate that the vicar himself should offer the bread, wine and lights for the Eucharist. Maldonatus,[44] however, relates that

[40] Concil. Elib. A.D. 305, Can. 28 ; Apostolic Constitutions, iii. 4. Statutes of the ancient Church [of Arles, A.D. 505] ap. Gratian, 1 Dist. xc. c. 2. According to Liturgia Armena tradotta (Venezia 1854) in the Armenian rite the offerings are presented by some chief-man of the people, by whom they are placed on a small side altar which stands to the right of the chief altar. There they remain until the deacon fetches them and presents them on the high altar. After the *Introit* a curtain is drawn whilst the offerings are being prepared. When it is withdrawn, the officiating priest is seen censing the altar.
[41] Pœnitential, i. xii. 4, A.D. 673, in Haddan and Stubbs, iii. 186.
[42] Gratian Causa xxxiii. Quaestio ii. c. 15.
[43] Decretals of Gregory, ix. Lib. v. tit. xvii. c. 2.
[44] De Ceremoniis Dissert. ii. sec. 17, no. 11.

in 1569 he found in some places offerings of bread and wine still
made as they are at this day in Milan.   Le Brun A.D. 1716 says
that in some parishes in the diocese of Riéz they offer at masses
for the dead a dish of meal, a loaf and a bottle of wine.   De
Moléon found the same practice existing at Rouen in 1698 ; and it
is said to have existed at Charlton in Wiltshire until it was
forbidden by Bishop Davenant in 1638.[45]

2. The preparation and presentation of the offering is the
deacon's part in the priestly office.[46]   Justin's account, it is true,
merely speaks of the prepared offering being brought in, but there
can be little doubt that those who brought it in and presented it
were the deacons.   They fulfilled the same function in the ninth
century.   A passage in the Epistle to the Colossians appears to
refer to this preparation, in which St. Paul, after saying that the
Body of Christ is the Church (i. 24), states that he has been made
the deacon of the Church "for the purpose of fulfilling the word of
God, to wit, the sacramental representation (μυστήριον) concealed
from bygone ages," and that his aim as such is (i, 28) " to present
every man to God in Christ as a perfect Christian," adding that
the sacramental representation is " Christ in you."   Ignatius also
(ad. Trall. c. 2) calls deacons ministers of the sacramental rep-
resentations (μυστήρια) of Jesus Christ.   The object of the deacon's
preparation, as we have already gathered from Cyprian's
letter,[47] is to make the offering upon which the Divine Spirit is
about to be invoked representative of a people united among
themselves as one body and united to Christ as their head.   So

<hr/>

[45] To Scudamore's Notitia Eucharistica I am indebted for the last
three references, and he appears to have derived them from Le Brun.

[46] Dionysius Areop. De Eccles. Hier. c. 3 : Chosen members of the
diaconal order with the presbyters place the sacred bread upon the divine
altar and the cup of blessing.

[47] Ep. 62, 13.   Augustin De Civitate Dei, xvii. 20, speaking of the
body prepared for Christ in the Eucharist says : Wherefore we recognise
the same voice of the Mediator speaking by prophecy in the 39th Psalm
[40th ; Heb. x. 5]   Sacrifice and offering Thou wouldest not, but a body
hast Thou prepared me."

Bishop Elfric of Winchester, A.D. 957 (Can. 37) says : " In the water is represented the people, but in the wine the Blood of Christ. When the water is mingled with the wine, the people is made one with Christ." The sixteenth Council of Toledo, A.D. 691, (Can. 6) therefore forbids priests to use unprepared bread, or, as it is expressed, any bread that comes to hand for the Eucharist, but to use only specially baked bread, circular in shape. At the present day in the Assyrian Church the Eucharistic bread is made from grain offered by all the members, which is first ground within the precincts of the church; the dough is then kneaded and leavened with the holy leaven, and baked by a presbyter and deacon while the earlier part of the service is being said.[48]

In the East, the preparation of the elements takes place at a previous service, known as the service of the πρόθεσις. In the Roman and Gallican Churches the oblation-loaves, which were offered ready baked since the fifth century, are enjoined to be specially baked. This rule practically placed the baking in the hands of the clergy. Hence in the year 787 A.D. Theodulf of Orleans is found enjoining upon his clergy (cap. 5) : " We charge you that the oblation which ye offer to God in that holy mystery be either baked by yourself or by your servants in your presence, and that ye take care that it be done in purity and chastity ; and that both the oblations and the wine and the water that belongs to the offering be provided and regarded with all purity and diligence and with the fear of God ; for there can be no mass-song without these three things, the oblation, the wine, and the water." Similar injunctions are given by William of Bleys in 1229 A.D.,[49] and by Peter Quivil of Exeter in 1287 A.D.[50] After this the proleptic honour bestowed in the Greek Church upon the prepared offering, or bread of presentation as it is

---

[48] Maclean's Catholicos of the East.
[49] Wilkins' Concilia, i. 623.
[50] *Ibid*, ii. 131.

called[51] becomes intelligible. For is it not then the mystical body
of Christ in visible representation (figura)[52] prepared to receive
the power of the Holy Ghost?

In the ninth century the deacon's duty of preparing the
offering had sunk to a minimum. It consisted in choosing a
sufficient number out of the oblation-loaves and placing them in
three or five rows upon the altar, and in mixing water with the
wine. At solemn mass the choosing of the oblation-loaves and the
mixing water with the wine were performed publicly and solemnly.
In private masses, however, where there was no deacon and the
priest himself had to discharge the deacon's duties, the choice of
the bread and the mixing water with the wine were done before
the service commenced, and in quasi-solemn masses, at any period
in the service when the priest found himself disengaged, such as
during the reading of the Epistle or the Gospel. This placing of
the prepared body on the altar by the deacon was technically called
presentation (ἀναφέρειν)[53] whereas the consecration by the presbyters was called offering (προσφέρειν). It seems, indeed, difficult now
to realise how important a part deacons played in the whole
ceremonial of the Eucharist before the creation of parishes under
single priests in the twelfth century, and the final abolition of
solemn masses. The deacon called to prayer and suggested to the
bishop or presbyter at every part of the service what to pray for.

---

[51] Theodori Poenit., i., xii., 3, in Haddan and Stubbs, iii. 186. Isidore
of Pelusium, A.D. 410, Ep. i. 123: We consecrate the bread of presentation
on white linen. Amalarius Praef. 2 in Lib. De Offic. Eccles. calls it *hostia*
or victim because it is destined to become the Body of Jesus Christ the
Victim. This destination is, he says, effected by the silent prayer of the
priest.

[52] Tertullian adv. Marcion iv. 40: A figure there could not be unless
there were first a veritable body. In the Armenian Liturgy, in the secret
prayer said by the priest at the bringing in of the oblation, he prays:
Receive with favourable eyes the gifts of the Church, by which not myrrh
and incense but Jesus Christ is offered our Saviour Who is represented
by these presents. Le Brun, iii. 185.

[53] Council of Ancyra, A.D. 314, in Gratian, 1 Dist. 4, c. 32, forbids an
apostate deacon to present ἀναφέρειν (the cup).

He dismissed the catechumens in order. He read out the names of the living who offered, and the dead for whom an offering was made. He held the chalice during the consecration-prayer, and at the proper time brought it into contact with the hallowed Oblation-loaves, thus ministerially consecrating it[54] He conducted the breaking of the Bread after consecration. He mixed the hallowed cup with unconsecrated wine in the communion bowl or scyphus before administering it to the people, took charge of the remains of the holy Elements, and carried the communion to the sick. In fact, with the exception of saying the three prayers,[55] there was no part of the service which did not pertain to him.

To show that this is no exaggerated view of the deacon's duties the epistle to Ludifred may be quoted[56] which is generally attributed to Isidore of Seville, or someone connected with him, in the seventh century :—

" It pertains (he writes) to deacons to assist presbyters and to minister in all things which are done in Christian sacraments . . . also to carry up the offerings and place them on the altar, to arrange and vest the Lord's table, to carry the cross, and to read aloud the Gospel . . .

To him, too, belongs the appointing of prayers and the calling over the names of those who offer. He proclaims ' Lift up your ears to the Lord.' He calls to prayers. He gives the peace, and announces the dismissal."

Similarly Elfric of Winchester A.D. 957 (Can. 17) :—The deacon is he that ministers to the mass-priest and places the oblations on the altar and reads the Gospel at the divine ministra-

---

[54] This explains the language of the Deacon Laurence to Pope Sixtus II. A.D. 257, quoted by Ambros. De Officiis, i. 41 : To whom, if I go away, will you entrust the consecration of the Lord's Blood. As Duchêsne, 448, observes : This action was only performed by a deacon when consecrating with his own bishop.

[55] Theodori Pœnit. ii. ii. 14, in Haddan and Stubbs, ii. 192. Deacons with the Greeks do not say the collect or the consecration-prayer (Dominus vobiscum), or the post-communion (completa). Duchêsne, p. 159.

[56] Gratian, 1 Dist. xxv. c. 1, sec. 7.

tion. He may baptize children and housel the people. They
ought to serve their Saviour in white albs and preserve the
heavenly life with purity.

It would appear, however, that sometime before the ninth century
a movement was in progress,[57] whereby the functions of the deacon
and of laymen were being concentrated in the hands of single presbyters, who vicariously discharging the priestly duties of all came to
to be exclusively called priests, and that at any rate in some places
very sordid motives were at the bottom of the encroachment. A
strong protest against this depression of the deacon's office is
extant, written by an anonymous Gallican writer,[58] who under the
pseudonym of Jerome, sets forth the deacon's duties as follows :—

" The deacons (he says), are they of whom we read in the
    Revelation, the seven angels of the Churches. These are
    the seven golden candlesticks, the seven voices of thunder
    . . . Without the deacon, the priest has only the name,
    but not the execution of the [priestly] office . . . The
    deacon is called God's minister . . . And as consecration is
    the priest's part, so the ministration of the sacrament
    belongs to the deacon . . . It is not lawful for priests
    to take the cup from the altar unless it is given them by a
    deacon. Almighty God has so arranged all things that he
    who thinks himself greater is less, and he who seems less is
    found to be greater. Consider only how true this is. Levites
    [i.e. deacons], place the offering on the altar. Levites pray
    before presbyters, so that bishops [= presbyters] if they
    are proud, see deacons preferred to themselves at God's

---

[57] A step in this direction was taken by Gregory, A.D. 594-604, at a
Roman Synod, who states (Gratian, 1 Dist. xcii., c. 2) that it is an ancient
but blameworthy custom of the Roman Church to make " deacons and
other persons engaged in the service of the altar lead the singing ; whence
it comes about that for promotion to the diaconate the voice is thought
more of than the character of the possessor. To remedy this, let deacons
for the future be forbidden to lead the singing and let them confine
themselves to their sacred ministry."

[58] Gratian, 1 Dist. xciii., c. 23.

altar . . . But, now, since avarice has grown up in the Church, as in the empire, the priest has lost the law, and the prophet the power of vision, and each one conjuring by the power of the episcopal name appropriates to himself all that belongs to Levites, not only claiming what is his of right, but all that belongs to all. The unfortunate [lower] clergy go begging in the streets, and, excluded from civil work, ask alms of whom they may."

In strict accordance with the view here propounded of the deacon's functions, when consecrations by single presbyters apart from the solemn service first became customary only oblation-loaves appear to have been consecrated at them ; for the Council of Orange A.D. 441 (Can. 17) found it necessary to pass a canon, ordaining that "The cup must be offered together with the box of oblation loaves, and be consecrated with the mixture proper for the Eucharist." A more important result followed when private masses in parochial oratories generally took the place of solemn Eucharists in the great collegiate churches. For since, by early rule, there is but one Eucharistic offering in every Church,[50] and a private or parochial mass is regarded not as an independent service, but as an integral part of the one solemn Eucharist detached from it for the convenience of a particular group of Christians, no deacon was needed at a private mass and consequently no provision was made for one in a parochial oratory. There was therefore at a private mass no solemn preparation of the offering and no one to give the cup to the people. Solemn masses being necessarily confined to the greater collegiate churches, it followed that at lesser churches where there were only private consecrations communion could only be given in one kind. This practise of communion in one kind continued even after parochial oratories had in the twelfth century been elevated to the position of cures of souls. A constitution of Archbishop Peckham A.D.

[50] Ignatius, ad Trall. c. 4 : Be earnest to use one Eucharist ; for there is one Flesh of our Lord, and one cup for uniting of His blood.

1281 ordains : In small churches it is allowed to none but them that celebrate to receive the Blood under the species of consecrated wine. Although, as Lyndwood[60] informs us, the cup was administered to the people in collegiate churches, more particularly in those of the Cistercians, down to the end of the fourteenth century, yet after the Council of Constance had decreed in 1415 A.D. that no change should be made in the received practice, what at first was a ceremonial necessity came in time to be regarded as a test of orthodoxy, and communion in one kind was adopted even in collegiate churches.[61] Solemn Eucharists became obsolete, and their place was taken by the quasi-solemn or high masses of mediæval times, in which the priest was not only the organ of united prayer, but the conductor of the whole service.

3. Although the heavenly offering which consecrates the Eucharist is made by the Great High Priest Himself, yet since it is procured by the prayers of the Church offered up in a collected form through its accredited representatives the presbyters,[62] it is usually spoken of as the presbyters' offering or προσφορά. Ignatius writing to the Trallians (c. 3) says " Apart from bishops, presbyters, and deacons, the body of the faithful cannot be called the Church," shewing that, however much laymen may offer and are indeed by virtue of their share in the royal priesthood authorized to make offerings to God as individuals,[63] yet that there can be no

[60] Provinciale, Oxford, 1679, p. 9.

[61] Cardinal Bona states that in his time in the Monastery of St. Denis all participated in both kinds and partook of the cup, using reeds (culami).

[62] In Rev. v. 8, the twenty-four presbyters present " the golden vials full of odours which are the prayers of saints."

[63] Tertullian Exhort. ad Cast. c. 7, writing when a Montanist : Are not even we laics priests ? It is written, A kingdom also and priests to God and His Father hath He made us. It is the authority of the Church which has established the difference between the presiding body and the laity, and the honour given by the formal seating has been hallowed by God. Where there is no formal seating of the presiding body [*i.e.*, out of Church and at home] you offer and baptise and are priest alone for yourself. But so soon as there are three, a Church is, albeit they are laics [and you have no power as a layman to make the offering of the Church].

consecration of the Body of Christ apart from the hierarchical orders. " God," says Justin in his dialogue with Trypho (c. 116), " receives offerings from no one except through His priests." Hence the eighteenth canon of the Council of Nicaea A.D. 325 speaks of presbyters as having the power of offering which deacons have not. And Jerome[64] says " It is the business of presbyters to procure by their prayers the coming of the Lord in the Eucharist."

Some difference of view, however, presents itself between the East and the West as to the way in which the offering of the Church is hallowed. Both the Eastern and the Western Churches teach that the agent in the hallowing is the Holy Ghost, who operates effectively in answer to the presbyters' prayers ; but whereas the Eastern Church emphasizes the descent of the Holy Ghost upon the prepared body, whereby it becomes the real Body of Christ, and prays for that descent in the so-called prayer of Epiclesis, the Western Church emphasizes the carrying of the earthly offering to heaven by Angels that it may be hallowed by being presented to the Father by the Son. Thus Irenaeus in the second century writes[65] : " Wherefore also the Lord promised to send the Comforter who should join us to God ; for as a loaf cannot possess unity unless fluid matter is with it, no more could we being many be made one in Christ without the water from heaven," which he explains to mean the Holy Ghost. And elsewhere[66] : " When the mingled cup and the prepared bread receive the Word of God, the Eucharist becomes the Body of Christ." Likewise Cyril of Jerusalem A.D. 347 in his instruction to catechumens says : " We beseech the merciful God to send the Holy Ghost upon the presented oblations that He may make the bread the Body of Christ, the wine the Blood of Christ." Similar language is also found in Augustine's

---

[64] Adv. Luciferanos, iv. 1672.
[65] Haer. iii. 17, 2.
[66] Haer. v. 2, 3.

sermons.[67]   The ordinary Western language is somewhat different.
The Roman canon, as it now stands, has this prayer : " Command
these things to be carried by the hand of Thy holy Angel to Thine
altar on high in the sight of Thy divine majesty, that so many as
shall partake at this altar of the most sacred Body and Blood of
Thy Son, may be filled with all heavenly grace and blessing."
The same words with the omission of the word *holy* before angel,
were in the canon of the ninth century.   In the canon as it existed
at the end of the fourth century the words were[68] : " We pray and
beseech Thee that Thou wilt receive this oblation to Thine altar
on high at the hands of Thy angels," where the plural angels
seems rather to refer to the seven spirits mentioned Rev. i. 4, and
iv. 5 (held by many to be the seven powers of the Holy Ghost[69])
which like deacons upon earth act as intermediaries between
heaven and earth rather than to the Holy Ghost Himself.[70]

4. There is a further point which deserves attention in
reference to the hallowing of the offering by the presbyters, viz.

---

[67] Serm. 227 : You [catechumens] were first ground by the humilia-
tion of fasting and the sacrament of exorcism. . . . The Holy Ghost comes
next. After the water the fire and you are made bread which is the Body
of Christ. Serm. 229 : After that you came to the water and were
moistened and made into one. The heat of the Holy Ghost was added
and you were baked and became the Lord's Bread. Serm. 271 : When
you were exorcised it was the grinding of you. When you were baptized
it was the moistening. When you received the fire of the Holy Ghost
it was the baking of you. Apost. Const. viii., 12.

[68] Duchêsne, 170. Apost. Const. viii., 13. Le Brun would place it
before 570 A.D. and after 400 A.D.

[69] Victorinus of Petau about 270 A.D. on the Revelation.   Possibly to
correspond with these seven powers the number of deacons was limited to
seven however large a city might be. Cornelius, A.D. 252, in Eusebius
Eccl. Hist. vi. 43 ; Concil. Neocaesar, A.D. 314, can. 14.

[70] In the Testament of the Twelve Patriarchs, about 130 A.D. the
Testament of Levi states that " in the sixth heaven are the angels of the
presence of the Lord, who minister and make propitiation to the Lord for
all the ignorances of the righteous ; and they offer to the Lord a season-
able sweet-smelling savour and a bloodless offering. And in the heaven
below this (the fifth) are the angels who bear the answers to the angels of
the presence of the Lord. And in the heaven next to this (the fourth)
are thrones and dominions in which hymns are ever offered to God.

that it was formerly performed as a corporate and collegiate act by all simultaneously in literal fulfilment of Christ's command "Do *ye* this in remembrance of Me," and also to ensure that unanimity in prayer which is essential to its being effective prayer.[71] Hence the concurrence of the bishop and presbyters is made by Ignatius the test of a valid Eucharist[72] In the Celtic Church of Iona it was the bishop's peculiar prerogative to consecrate the Eucharist without the assistance of other presbyters.[73] Usually this concurrence was given by the presbyters standing round whilst the bishop said the prayer of hallowing,[74] and responding Amen at its close, and such appears to have been the Eastern[75] and the Gallican use.[76] Nevertheless, at some very early time another practise existed or was introduced at Rome, out of which have grown the multiplied private masses of the Latin Church.[77] The Liber Pontificalis refers to it by this curious entry : "Zephyrinus [200-218] established the custom of holding patens of glass before the presbyters and for deacons to hold them whilst the bishop

[71] Cyprian, De Orat. Dom., c. 8 : The Master of prayer would not have prayer to be made singly and individually. De Unit. Eccl., c. 12 ; Theodulf, A.D. 787, cap. 7 : Christ's promise was not made to individuals, but to two or three gathered together in His name. Dionysius, A.D. 532, De Eccl. Hier. c. 3 : Then the sacred ministers of sacred things contemplate in all purity the most holy mystery and celebrate in a universal Hymn of Praise to the Author and Giver of all good. That hymn some call a Hymn of Praise ; others the symbol [or sacramental expression] of worship ; but others more correctly a hierarchical thanksgiving.

[72] Ad Trall. c. 6. Cyprian, Ep. 4 (Oxf. 5), 2, allows a single presbyter to offer with the confessors to preserve peace.

[73] Warren's Celtic Church, 128.

[74] Synod of Rome under Victor, A.D. 196, commonly called the Canons of Hippolytus : When a bishop celebrates the synaxis let the presbyters stand by him clothed in white.

[75] Apost. Const., viii., 12.

[76] Pseudo-Isidore in Gratian, iii. Dist. i. c. 59 : On the more solemn days let a bishop have seven, or five, or three deacons . . And let the presbyters stand right and left and give consent to his sacrifice.

[77] Leo, A.D. 440-461, Ep. 11, nevertheless enjoins : As often as an influx of fresh people fills the collegiate church in which the Eucharist is celebrated (basilicam in qua agitur), so often let another sacrifice be offered.

celebrated mass standing upright by him." The meaning of these
words (which are not altogether clear) appears to be that whereas
before the time of Zephyrinus the bishop consecrated the whole of
the offering with the presbyters' assent, Zephyrinus introduced the
practise for each of the presbyters to consecrate a separate portion
of it which a deacon held before him on a paten of glass. Whether[78]
this be the origin or not of separate simultaneous consecrations
instead of one consecration by the prayers of all (which is the
Eastern use),[79] or whether the practise dates back to apostolic
times and is a survival of that followed by the two apostles St.
Peter and St. Paul when at Rome, or whether it was introduced by
St. Clement at the fusion of the Jewish and Gentile elements in
that Church, it was certainly the regular custom in the time of
Innocent I. (A.D. 404-416). For that Pope writing to Decentius
informs him that on ordinary liturgical days the presbyters consecrated with their bishop, but that on Sundays when they were
engaged in their titles he was in the habit of sending to them
consecrated Loaves by the hands of collets that they might not
even on that day be deprived of communion with himself ; he could
not, however, do the same for presbyters in the country because
"the sacraments may not be carried about far." According to
Duchêsne some of the presbyters of whom there were then fifty[80]
must even in the fifth century have consecrated privately in the
twenty-five titular Churches, and consecrated Loaves were sent to
them as the *Fermentum* for the commixture. On the other hand
the Jesuit De Smedt denies that private consecrations were
practised so early and considers that the consecrated Loaves were
sent to them for the communion of the people. In the sixth
century co-consecration by the bishop and presbyters was the

[78] Duchêsne, 167.
[79] Bona Lib. i., c. 18, sec. 9.
[80] Cornelius, A.D. 252, in Euseb. vi. 43, states that there were 46.   It
is supposed that there were some vacancies and that two presbyters were
attached to each title. The number of titular Churches which was 25 in the
third century was not increased till the twelfth century when there were 28

ordinary Roman practise[61] ; but the canons passed in the Gallican
Church, requiring country presbyters not to hold service in the
country on the greater festivals but to repair to their collegiate
churches for solemn consecrations[62] shew either that co-consecrations
were not then in use in Gaul or that considerations of convenience
were already disintegrating solemn mass and preparing the way for
the single-handed parochial masses of the twelfth and succeeding
centuries. The Celtic rule forbidding a single presbyter to consecrate without at least one other presbyter to co-operate appears
to have been generally prevalent in this country in the seventh
century ; for Archbishop Theodore found it necessary to rule[63]
that " It is lawful for single presbyters to celebrate masses." In
the eighth and ninth centuries collegiate consecration had become
unusual except at the high festivals of Christmas, the Epiphany,
Holy Easter and the following day, the Lord's Ascension, Pentecost and the Festival of St. Peter and St. Paul,[64] and its place was
taken by a number of successive consecrations each performed by
a single presbyter at a separate altar, oratory or chapel. Three
centuries later even the principal service of a collegiate church
followed the custom of a private mass, and ceased to be celebrated
solemnly except at an ordination or the consecration of a Church.[65]
Thus the one great solemnity of offering, thanksgiving, meditation,
and propitiation at which the whole Church present and absent
took part directly and by visible signs became split up into a series
of services of private devotion, and the term priest (sacerdos),
which had hitherto been confined to the bishop as the embodiment
of the priestly powers of the Church, was applied to every presby-

[61] Duchêsne, 167.

[62] Council of Agde, A.D. 506, Can. 21, in Gratian, iii. Dist. i. c. 55 ;
Can. 27 of Council of Orléans, A.D. 511, *Ibid*, iii. Dist. iii. c. 5 ; Can. 7 of
Council of Tarracon, A.D. 516 ; and Can. 6 of Council of Arverne, A.D. 535.

[63] Pœnit. II. ii. 7, in Haddan and Stubbs, iii. 191.

[64] Duchêsne, 444.

[65] Bona, Lib. i. c. 18, sec. 9, nevertheless relates that at the obsequies
of Philip Augustus of France there were two simultaneous consecrations.

ter who consecrated alone as having a cure of souls.[66] Since the
Constitution of Pious V. *Quo primum tempore* in 1568 santioning
the rite, and that of Clement VIII. *Cum novissime* in 1600
sanctioning the ceremonial, private masses solemnly performed are
the only ones authoritatively sanctioned within the Roman
obedience, except where ancient usage has not been interrupted
during the previous two hundred years.

5. The hallowing of the offering was completed by the
fraction and the Lord's Prayer, the Lord's Prayer being regarded
as the great collect summing up all the preceding prayers.[67]
Originally the Lord's Prayer preceded the fraction, and it is stated
to have been the only prayer at which in the earliest times the
consecration of the offering was effected,[68] but it was transferred
by Gregory the Great, 590-604 A.D. to a place after the fraction.
The fraction itself was a very complicated ceremony in churches
of the Gallican rite, its object being apparently not merely to
divide the hallowed Loaf for subsequent distribution—which
naturally involved a greater amount of division on greater festivals
—but also to enable the officiant to lay out the Particles upon the
corporal in some fanciful picture of the Lord's Body. The most
elaborate fraction was that used in the Irish Church, varying from
a division into five parts prescribed for ordinary days to a division

---

[66] Le Brun, i. 662, note has shown that for the first six centuries the
term " sacerdos " applied exclusively to the bishop. In the two following
centuries it was applied to the bishop and to the presbyter who represented
him indifferently ; in the ninth century to all presbyters having a cure of
souls.

[67] Concil. Aurel. iii. A.D. 538, Can. 29, forbids anyone of the faithful
to leave the church until the Lord's Prayer has been said, evidently
regarding this prayer as the great summing-up prayer, without which
previous prayers were incomplete.

[68] Gregory, Ep. ix. 10: We therefore say the Lord's Prayer soon after
the invocation (precem), because it was the custom of the Apostles to
consecrate the oblation loaf only at that prayer. Walafrid Strabo, c. 22.
Mabillon, Mus. Ital. ii. 566, no. 7, states that the Lateran Church in the
twelfth century used no collects, and consecrated by only using the Lord's
Prayer.

into sixty-five parts which was prescribed for Ascension Day.[80] The simpler ceremonial of the Roman Church was opposed to excessive division, and probably led to the prohibition of making fanciful pictures with the Particles in the Gallican Church.[90] Whether the Mozarabic use of dividing the hallowed Loaf into nine particles and laying out seven in the form of a cross, reserving two others for the officiant's communion and the commixture respectively,[91] was peculiar to the Spanish Church or was the early Roman practise adopted after 567, it is now impossible to say. The mediæval Roman use was, as is well known, a fraction into three parts only, but this use derives its authority from Pope Sergius I. in 687 A.D. and appears to have been prescribed for each presbyter as the minimum for ceremonial use ; one part dipped in the cup representing Christ alive from the dead, the second consumed by the priest, Christ walking about on earth, the third reserved, signifying Christ's Body resting in the tomb,[92] As conducted in the ninth century by the deacons, after the pope had broken off the crown of one Loaf every bishop and presbyter present breaking two consecrated Loaves which were held before him by a collet, it must

[80] Stowe Missal, p. 10.

[90] Second Council of Tours, A.D. 567, Can. 3 : That the Lord's Body be not laid out upon the altar in a fanciful form (imaginario ordine) but only in the form of a cross. Dr. Rock, however, renders imaginario ordine " among the images ! " See also letter of Pelagius I. A.D. 558, to Sapandus, Archbishop of Arles, in Jaffé, p. 978. Mabillon De Liturg. Gall. I. c. 9, holds the view given in the text.

[91] Three, called respectively Death, Birth, Resurrection, represented the arms and centre. Above the central Birth a fourth was placed called Incarnation, and below it three called respectively Circumcision, Apparition, Passion. The remaining two, called Kingdom and Glory, were reserved for the Priest's Communion and the Sancta. Duchêsne, 209.

[92] Gratian, iii. Dist. ii. c. 22. According to Florus, Deacon of Lyons, it was the teaching of Amalarius that Christ had a threefold body, viz. : 1, the body which He assumed of the Virgin ; 2, His body which consists of the members of the Church who are at any time alive ; and 3, His body consisting of Members of the Church who are at rest. This he alleged as the reason for dividing the consecrated Host into 3 parts, one to be placed in the chalice for Christ, a second to be consumed by the living, a third to be placed on the altar for the dead.

have been a fraction into a large number of particles.

VI. The Communion.

1. The last point mentioned by Justin is the communion. One feature preparatory to the communion must, however, first be noticed, viz. (1) the ceremony of the *Sancta* or pre-Consecrated Elements, which is, in fact, part of the communion— the communion with the saints of other times; and (2) the kindred ceremony of the *Fermentum* or leaven, which is the communion with the saints of other places. The ceremony of the Sancta, which belongs only to solemn mass, consists in placing in the cup a portion of the pre-consecrated Loaf reserved from the last solemn mass, in order that by the commixture all who partake of the cup may be brought into communion with all who offered at the previous solemn mass, and through them with all who have been in the communion of the Church from the beginning.[93] The ceremony of the *Fermentum* is similar, but it appears to belong to private and non-solemn mass. It consisted in placing in the cup a portion of the Loaf consecrated by the bishop at solemn mass to serve as a connecting link between those who communicate at a private mass and those who offered at the solemn mass.[94] As now practised, the commixture is a distinct ceremony and not a mere survival of the *Fermentum*, its object being to represent the Body of Christ in its glorified resurrection-state through the infusion of the Blood which is the life unto the

---

[93] 1 Cor. x. 17. Le Brun iii. 189, suggests that out of this practice of carrying the pre-sanctified Host to the altar together with the unconsecrated offerings may have arisen the devotion now paid in the East to the prepared offering itself.

[94] Liber Pontificalis in Vita Melchiadis : This pope ordained that consecrated Oblations should be sent to the different churches from the bishop's consecration.

Crucified Body.[95] The *Fermentum* perpetuated the great feature of solemn mass, which is not only that at it all offer, but that all offer as a united Body, the one mystical Body of Christ, the Church of all time (1 Tim., ii., 2). If a private mass is offered it is for some private group or limited circle of Christians, whereas solemn mass is the offering made by all and for all in which the communion of saints is fully realized. " The Eucharist (says St. Chrysostom[96]) is made on behalf of the world, of those who have gone before and of those who are to follow after." In the Mozarabic rite the chief officiant says[97] : " Our priests (*i.e.* bishops) offer to the Lord God, the Roman pope and the rest for themselves and for all clergy and people entrusted to their charge and for the whole fraternity. Also the presbyters, deacons, clergy and people offer in honour of the saints for themselves and those belonging to them ; " to which the people respond " They offer for themselves and the whole fraternity." In the Stowe Missal the offering is made " for all who rest who have gone before us in the Lord's peace from Adam to the present day, whose names are known to God." In the Blickling Homilies[98] the same idea is thus expressed : " The bishop and the priest if they will rightly serve God . . . must at least once a week sing mass for all Christian people and for all who have been from the beginning of the world . . . And those that are in heaven shall intercede for those who are engaged in this song. And they shall be in the prayer of all earthly folks who have been Christians or yet may be." It was at this solemn moment when by the commixture of the preconsecrated

---

[95] Amalarius De Eccles. Offic. iii. 31 : In that office (the commixture) is shewn the returning of the Blood shed for our soul and of the Flesh put to death for our body to their proper substance and the growing of them into the new Man through the life-giving Spirit, which will die no more, which has died for us and has risen again. Missal Maurilla Episc. Rotom. et Joannes Abricensis De Offic. p. 23 : By the l'article of the Ubble dropped into the cup is indicated the Body of Christ which has risen from the dead.

[96] Hom. 24, in Math.

[97] Duchêsne, 199.

[98] Early English Text Society.

Loaf in the cup the communion of the saints of all time was con-
summated that the great blessing, the so-called triple benediction,
was in the Gallican Church given by the bishop to the people.[99]

From this conception of the Eucharist it was a logical
corollary that when private consecrations for particular groups of
Christians, at which there was no commixture with the Eucharist
of other days, took the place of solemn offerings made by all
and for all, private consecrations for the dead, which were at
first exceptional services,[100] should be introduced as their regular
complement ; and that when private masses solemnly celebrated
had become everywhere the rule, as was the case in the thirteenth
century, private masses for the dead should be required to be also
solemnly celebrated wherever a sufficient number of priests were
available for the purpose.[101]

2. As simultaneous consecration is one of the great features
of solemn mass, so simultaneous participation is another feature
which characterizes the communion. The pontiff first communicated himself in both kinds. He then gave the Eucharistic Bread
into the hands of all the bishops and presbyters present, who
repairing to the altar, placed their right hands upon it at the
north side and partook simultaneously. He next gave the
Eucharistic Bread to the deacons, who in like manner repaired to
the altar, and placing their hands upon it at the south side partook
simultaneously. It seems not improbable that this manner of

---

[99] The fourth Council of Toledo, A.D. 633, Can. 18 : Some priests communicate directly after the Lord's Prayer and afterwards give the benediction to the people ; instead of which . . we decree that the solemn
benediction be given immediately after the fraction when the Particle
has been placed in the cup.

[100] Tertullian, Exhort. ad Cas. c. 11, states that it was the custom to
make an offering for the dead annually on their birthdays. Cyprian, Ep.
65 (Oxf. 1), 2, A.D. 249 : It is not allowed that any offering be made by
you for his repose nor any prayer be made in Church in his name.
Theodori, Pœnit. II. v. 2, in Haddan and Stubbs, iii. 194 : On the 1st, 3rd,
9th and 30th days let mass be said for the dead, and again after a year if
they wish let the same course be followed.

[101] Honorius III, A.D. 1217, in Decret. Lib. iii. tit. xli. c. 11.

partaking with the hand placed upon the altar after the Eucharist had been received may have been the usual manner for all to partake in early times, and, being the Christian equivalent of the taking of the military oath, first obtained for the Eucharist the name of *sacramentum*.[102] This view would also explain the language of Cornelius in the third century, who thus describes the action of his rival Novatus[103] : "Having made the oblation (προσφορά, *i.e.*, the consecration) and distributed a part to each one, he compels the unhappy man to swear instead of giving thanks, holding the hands of the receiver with both his own and not letting them go until he has sworn in these words, for I shall repeat the very words : 'Swear to me by the Body and Blood of our Saviour that you will never desert me nor turn to Cornelius.'" Optatus of Milevis, remonstrating with the Donatists (vi., 93) in the fifth century for their desecration of Catholic altars, says ; "What is there so sacrilegious as to break, scrape, remove the altars of God ? . . . whereon the vows of the people and the members of Christ have been borne ?" Long before the ninth century this practise had become obsolete and the communion was first given to the principal laity and to women in their places in church by the bishop and deacon. The rest then came forward into the choir and were communicated with the Lord's Body by the bishop or some one of the presbyters, and partook of the cup through a *pugillaris, calamus* or reed at the hands of one of the assisting deacons.[104] This was called "being confirmed."

There was, however, some difference made in the manner of communicating the different classes, in that the single consecrated chalice was used only for the higher clergy. Its contents were mixed with unconsecrated wine in the communion bowls (scyphi) for the communion of the people, and out of these were replenished

---

[102] Tertullian, De Idol. c. 19 : There is no agreement between the divine and the human oath of fidelity. See Pliny, letter x. 96.

[103] Euseb. vi. 43.

[104] Mabillon, Mus. Ital. ii. 14.

the lesser bowls (fontes) as they were wanted, a portion of the
hallowed Loaf having been first put into each. Women, moreover,
were not allowed to receive the consecrated bread direct into their
hands—which may possibly have been ruled to prevent such
abuses as those practised by the Gnostic Marcus[105]—but the
Eucharist was either placed directly in their mouths, as the
Council of Rouen in 650 A.D. (Can. 2) authorised, probably
following the Roman practise, or they received it on a napkin
called the Lord's napkin or the housel-towel, as was ordered by the
Gallican Council of Auxerro in 578 A.D. (Can. 36). In this connection it seems a curious irony that the use of the housel-towel
continued at St. Mary's, Oxford, until it was done away with by
Cardinal Newman when he was vicar of the parish, the housel-
towels being finally disposed of by him in 1869.[106]

When the service of the ninth century is compared with that
of the twelfth or the fifteenth centuries, it is at once seen that,
although it was a service rendered with great ceremonial splendour,
it retained all the simpler features of the earliest times. Before
all things it was a visibly corporate and collegiate act. Each of
the three classes acknowledged by the Church had its own separate
share therein, which it discharged personally and not vicariously.
The laity provided the materials for the great act wherein by
means of sacramental signs they surrendered themselves to God
(Rom., xii., 1). The deacon conducted the ceremonial and prepared the people's offerings, thus taking from them their individual
character and moulding them into one to represent the earthly
Church a united body. The presbyters by their prayers procured
the descent of the Holy Ghost upon the prepared body whereby it
became a means of grace to the partakers. The ceremonial
functions of the bishop were confined to receiving the offerings,
and giving the communion, his intercessory functions to saying

[105] Irenæus, i. 13 ; Hippolytus, vi. 34.
[106] Guardian, 18 February, 1891. I am reminded that as Newman's
connection with St. Mary's ceased some twenty-five years previously,
they must have been removed by him long before.

the collect, the consecration-prayer, and the post-communion. Even in the time of Gregory VII. in the eleventh century the three prayers were still the prominent feature, but a change was taking place ; for, says Micrologus,[107] speaking of the different parts of the service, " only one collect is properly said before the readings commence, and it is so called because the presbyter who acts for the people sums up and concludes in it the antecedent prayers of all. Nevertheless, this rule is now little heeded. Many weary and distract those present by introducing a multiplicity of prayers, which so long as they are approved prayers are allowed, but their number is limited to seven, so as never to exceed the number of petitions in the Lord's Prayer." Similarly he mentions the canon and the post-communion collect, but no other prayers. All other prayers seem to have been in his day additions made at the private discretion of the priest.

In the Frankish Empire Pepin attempted, and his son Charles, in the year 789 A.D. succeeded, in abolishing to a great extent the old Gallican uses,[108] the Roman rite (*i.e.* the rite then practised at Rome, not the present Roman rite) being ordered to be everywhere introduced in its place. The enactment seems to have been singularly unpopular with both clergy and people. New orders and sacramental books were indeed made purporting to be copies of or to represent the Roman rite, but the prayers and the ritual dear to the people were retained in them and inserted as being Roman usages. For instance, ordination took place first with the imposition of hands and the two prayers peculiar to the Roman rite, but there followed the Gallican form of imposition of hands with chrism, and the three prayers peculiar to the Gallican rite. Eventually the mixed Gallican ritual became the ritual of Rome. Nicolaus I. in 864 says that chrism was not used in ordinations at Rome in his day. Innocent III. in 1215 says that it was used everywhere. In the ninth century the Roman use was to make the sign of the

---

[107] c. 3 in Migne Patrol, cli. 979.
[108] Duchêsne, p. 97 ; Batiffol, p. 81.

cross six times in the canon. Innocent III. say that it was made twenty-five times in his time, apparently in accordance with the Gallican Roman ceremonial.

The reference of everything to the bishop in the distinctly Roman order of St. Amand may possibly have been intended to check the habit of following Gallican uses ; for since the inferior clergy and the laity could not be trusted to abstain from indigenous uses if left to themselves, no step was allowed to be taken by them without the bishop's nod of approval.   The nod of approval became in the following centuries the prescribing the general conduct of the whole service by the bishop or by one whom he delegated to represent himself.   Thus diocesan conformity was secured, and ritual was reduced to a state of feudal dependence.   Since then feudalism has asserted itself in every department of life and spared neither the Church nor its government.   Perhaps it was once necessary that it should be so, or there might have been an end of all unity ; but feudalism is no longer necessary now.   Socialism is once more in the air, and half the Christian world is embittered against any vicarious exercise of that priesthood which it is rightly claimed belongs to all the people of God collectively.   Is it not possible that in the obsolete usages of solemn mass may be found the ritual expression of that true Christian socialism which it should be the object of us all to promote ?   If so, can the manner of solemnly offering the Eucharist in the ninth and preceding centuries at Rome and elsewhere be only a matter of archæological interest ? Might not the revival of it be one of the greatest aids towards re-uniting divided Christendom ?

APPENDIX.

THE ORDER OF ST. AMAND.

In the name of our Lord Jesus Christ. Here beginneth the order[109] according to which mass is celebrated in the holy apostolical Church of Rome, which we have taken great care and pains [to describe], not always grammatically but correctly, using plain
5 language ; in other words, the manner in which the pontiff proceeds on a solemn day with high honour ; according as it has been ascertained from the holy fathers.

1. PREPARATION.

First of all the whole clergy and people go forth to the church where mass is to be said,[110] and the pontiff enters the sacristy and
10 puts on his sacerdotal vestments. When he wears dalmatics, the deacons also wear them and the subdeacons wrap themselves in amices (anagolagium) round the neck and put on white tunics such as they have made either of linen or of silk. If the pontiff does not wear dalmatics neither deacons nor subdeacons wrap themselves in
15 amices, but walk in white tunics and planets. Whilst the pontiff sits in the sacristy in his seat, the deacon who is about to read has charge of the Gospel-book. He afterwards gives it to the sub-deacon. The subdeacon then carries it up the centre to the sanctuary (presbyterium), and no one thinks of keeping his seat
20 when he is seen coming ; and passing up the subdeacon lays it on the altar. Meantime the fourth (see below, line 248) in the choir (scola) stands before the pontiff and says to the subdeacon of the district, " So and so will sing the responsory ; So and so the Alleluia." Then the pontiff gives the word to the choir, " Move

---

[109] The Order is the ceremonial directory. The Sacramentary contains the prayers used by the pontiff, but usually not those for the deacon.

[110] Solemn mass was said in the several churches according to their dignity, it being arranged that it should be said in nearly all once a year.

25 forward ! "   And he passes word back to the choir-head,[111] " Give
your orders."   Then the aforesaid subdeacon comes round and
whispers into the pontiff's ear, " So and so will read ; So and so
will sing."

2. Processional Entrance. Introit.

Then the almoner[112] lights two [large] wax candles (cereos)
30 outside the sacristy to light the pontiff, which is the custom at all
times, and he enters before the pontiff and places them behind the
altar (retro altare) in two candlesticks (candelabra) right and left.
Then the collets light tapers (cereostata) outside the sacristy and
the pontiff issues from the sacristy together with the deacons, two
35 supporting him right and left, and seven tapers are carried before
him, and the subdeacon of the day[113] (? temperita) walks before the
pontiff with a censer.   The deacons wear planets over their
dalmatics until they have come with the pontiff to the
sanctuary end (summum presbyterium).   And when they have
40 entered they take off their planets and their assistants (ministri)
take charge of them.   When the subdeacon who is head of the
choir sees them taking off their planets and the pontiff entering
the sanctuary, he also takes off his planet and a choir-collet takes
charge of it.   Then the priests (sacerdotes) rise and stand.   The
45 subdeacons who enter before the pontiff do not pass up through the
centre of the choir (scola), but remain standing right and left
below the screen (cancellus) on each side.   And when the pontiff
has approached the choir (scola) these stand, the collets with the
tapers in reverse order the last first.   Passing with his deacons
50 through the centre of the choir (scola) the pontiff nods to the
head of the choir to say the *Gloria*.   The senior bishop and the

[111] It appears from line 41 that the subdeacon of the district was the
head of the choir for the time being.

[112] He is called the subdeacon-almoner below, line 146.

[113] It appears from line 120 that he was not the subdeacon of the
district.

senior presbyter then come up. The pontiff gives them the *Peace,*
and then gives it to the deacons. If the pontiff be not present
the *Peace* is given in a similar manner by the deacon who will read
55 the Gospel that day. Then he advances (psallit)[114] before the altar
and stands with bared head and the deacons likewise. When the
choir have sung *As it was in the beginning,* the deacons rise from
prayer and kiss the altar on both sides. And when the choir have
sung the verse for repetition[115] the pontiff rises from prayer and
60 kisses the Gospel-book upon the altar and passes from the right
side of the altar to his seat and the deacons with him on either
side standing and facing eastwards.

3. Kyries, Gloria in Excelsis, Collect.

Then the collets place the tapers which they carry on the
ground ; and when the choir have completed the anthem, the
65 pontiff nods for the *Lord have mercy* to be said. The choir say it
and the district officials (regionarii) standing below the reading
desk (ambo) repeat it. After the third repetition he again nods
for the *Christ have mercy* to be said. After it has been said for
the third time he once more nods for the *Lord have mercy* to be
70 said. And when the nine times are completed he nods for a finish
to be made. Turning towards the people the pontiff then begins
Glory to God in the highest, and then turns round to the East and
the deacons with him until it is finished. When it is finished,
turning to the people, he says, *Peace be with you.* They reply,
75 *And with thy spirit.* Then, *Let us pray.* Then the collets take
up their tapers and place them before the altar in the order which

---

[114] Duchêsne renders it thus.

[115] This is part of the extract called the anthem in line 64. Mabillon,
Liturg. Gall. i. 5, states that an antiphonary included introits. Batiffol
Histoire du Bréviaire, p. 54, states that in the language of the eighth
century *antiphonarium* meant a collection of the parts which were sung
at *mass,* which are now called *Liber Gradualis,* not the parts which were
sung at *matins,* which latter were contained in the *Liber Responsalis.*

they hold. [And the pontiff says the collect after silent prayer.]

4. THE EPISTLE, GRADUAL AND ALLELUIA.

The collect being concluded the pontiff sits in his seat and
the deacons stand on either side. And the choir go back below
80 the platform (tabula) which is below the reading-desk (ambo), and
the subdeacons who stand below the screen (cancellus) come
(psallunt) round the altar on both sides. The pontiff gives the
signal for the priests in the sanctuary (presbyterium) to be seated.
Then a lesson is read by the subdeacon in the reading-desk, *stans*
85 *in medium de scola aut acolitus planeta,*[116] and he receives the
gradual (cantarium) and advances to the reading-desk and says
the responsory ; similarly another says the *Alleluia.*

5. THE GOSPEL.

This over, the deacon bows to the pontiff and the pontiff gives
order for the Gospel to be read. [The deacon] then goes to the
90 altar, kisses the Gospel-book and takes it up. Then the pontiff
rises from his seat and all the priests also stand. And there walk
in front of him [the deacon] two subdeacons, one on the right, the
other on the left, and two collets carrying before him two tapers.
And when [the deacon] comes below the reading desk, the subdeacon
95 on his right holds up before him his left arm and the deacon places
the Gospel-book upon it until he receives the sign. Then he advances
to the reading-desk, and the tapers are placed before the reading-
desk and the Gospel is read. The subdeacon then receives the

---

[116] As they stand these words have no meaning. Mabillon's Order is
as follows : The subdeacon mounts the reading desk and reads. After
he has read, a singer with the gradual mounts it and says the response.
Duchêsne suggests that some words must have dropped out, and that the
corrupt passage may mean that the singer laid aside his planet before
mounting the reading desk for the response.

Gospel-book and holds it on his breast below the reading-desk
100 until all have kissed it. He then replaces it in its box. The
deacon returns to the altar and the tapers before him which are
placed behind the altar and also the other tapers. And if there is
a cloth (pallium) upon the altar he folds it up in one place to the
East and the body-cloth (corporale) is spread over the altar by the
105 deacons.

6. The People's Offering.

Then the pontiff washes his hands and rises from his seat, and
the choir go back to the left (north) side of the sanctuary (presbyterii).
Then the pontiff comes down to receive oblations from the people
and the archdeacon nods to the choir to commence the offertory
110 anthem. And as the pontiff receives the [oblation-loaves] he hands
them to a subdeacon, who places them on a linen cloth (sindon)
carried by collets behind him. The deacons receive the cruets
(amulas) of wine. The [large] chalice for station days (stationarius)
is carried by the subdeacon of the district, and the deacon empties
115 the cruets into the holy chalice itself, and when it is full it is
emptied into the bowl (scyphus) carried by collets. Then the
pontiff passes with the deacons to the side of the women and they
do likewise. Then he returns to his seat, the deacons continuing
to receive cruets. Meantime there stand before the pontiff the
120 precentor, the succentor, notaries and district-officials, whilst the
presbyters are receiving oblation-loaves and cruets within the
choir as well from the side of the men as of the women, and collets
hold linen cloths and bowls (scyphi) to get them together.

7. Preparation of the Offering.
Offerings of the Clergy.

Then the archdeacon washes his hands and goes before the
125 altar and the other deacons wash their hands and the collets hold

the linen cloth (sindon) with the oblation-loaves which the pontiff
has received from the people at the right [south] corner of the
altar and a choice is made from them by the subdeacon of the day
(? temperita) and he gives them [those which he has chosen] to the
130 subdeacon of the district (regionarius),[117] who hands them to the
archdeacon, who places them in three or five ranks upon the altar,
enough to suffice for the people and to remain over till the morrow,
according to the canonical regulation.   Meanwhile the chalice is
held by the subdeacon of the district, and the archdeacon receives
135 the pontiff's cruet at the hands of his almoner and empties it into
the holy chalice and similarly the cruets of the presbyters and the
deacons.   Then the subdeacon holds a strainer over the chalice
and wine is poured through it, of that which the people offered
which is in the bowl (scyphus).   Then a member of the choir
140 brings a small water bowl (fons) full of clean water and hands it
to the almoner, and the almoner hands it to the archdeacon, who
pours it in the form of a cross into the holy chalice, held by the
subdeacon at the right corner of the altar.   Then the pontiff
comes down from his seat and comes before the altar, and the
145 archdeacon receives the pontiff's oblation-loaves at the hand of the
subdeacon-almoner and he hands them to the pontiff and the
pontiff places them on the altar.   The archdeacon then takes the
chalice from the subdeacon and places it upon the altar.

8.   The Consecration.

The pontiff nods to the choir to stop, and they withdraw
150 below the platform (tabula).   On the Lord's Nativity, Epiphany,

---

[117] There were previously to the twelfth century 25 titles (tituli) at
Rome, which in some respects resembled parish-churches. Each of these
was under the care of two presbyters. Independently of this division
Rome was divided into 7 districts (regiones) of administration for the care
of the poor, orphans, hospitals and other ecclesiastical philanthropies,
each of which was presided over by a deacon, who had a subdeacon and
collets to assist him. It was a very much later idea that the deacon of a
district should be attached to some title.

Holy Sabbath, Holy Easter (Dominica), and the following day (feria secunda), the Lord's Ascension, Pentecost, and the birthday of St. Peter and St. Paul, the bishops take up a position behind the pontiff with bowed heads and the presbyters on either side of him,

155 and each one holds a body-cloth in his hand. Two oblation-loaves are then given to each one by the archdeacon, and the pontiff says the canon so that it can be heard by them, and they hallow the oblation-loaves, which they hold as the pontiff does. [The deacons meanwhile stand] with bowed head behind the bishops, and sub-

160 deacons in front of the pontiff with bowed heads towards the altar until he comes to the words, *To us sinners also.* But if it be not a solemn day, so soon as the chalice is placed upon the altar the presbyters return to the sanctuary (presbyterium) and the rest of the clergy go back below the platform; and if it be a Sunday the

165 presbyters stand with bowed heads, but on ordinary days they kneel when the *Holy, Holy* commences. And the collets come and stand before the altar behind the deacons right and left, girt about with linen cloths (sindones). And one of them girt about with a silken cloth (palla),[118] embroidered with a cross, holds the paten

170 on his breast standing in front, and others hold bowls great and small (scyphos cum fonte), others sacks. And when the pontiff comes to the words *All honour and glory*, he takes up the two oblation-loaves in his hands, and the deacon holding the chalice raises it slightly until he says,[119] *World without end. Amen.*

9. The Blessing and the Fraction.

175 Then they all rise from prayer, both deacons and priests (sacerdotes), and when the pontiff has said, *May the Lord's peace*

---

[118] Both the sindon and the palla are altar coverings, which the collets appear to assume as being temporary altars.

[119] The Ordo in Muratori I. 985, has a slightly different version: When the pontiff comes to the words, *Through Him and with Him*, the archdeacon takes up the chalice with the offering-cloth (offertorium) passed through the handles, and holding it raises it towards the pontiff. . . . The pontiff then touches the side of it with the oblation loaves.

be ever with you,[120] the sub-deacon takes the paten from the collet and hands it to the archdeacon, and he holds it at the pontiff's right hand whilst the [pontiff] breaks one of the oblation-

180 loaves which he offered for himself and leaves the crown of it upon the altar, and he places one whole one and the remaining half (aliam mediam) in the paten, and the archdeacon returns the paten to the collet and the pontiff goes back to his seat. Then other deacons break the Bread in the paten and bishops also on

185 the right side of the apse (abside). Then the archdeacon takes up the chalice from the altar and gives it to the subdeacon, and stands with him at the right corner of the altar, and collets advance (psallunt) to the altar[121] with sacks and stand about the altar, and the archdeacon places oblation-Loaves in every sack, and

190 they return to the presbyters for them to break them, presbyters and deacons meanwhile singing in an undertone (secreto) *Blessed are the undefiled.* Should necessity occur, the oblation-Loaves are first divided by a presbyter and afterwards broken by the sub-deacons of the districts. The choir then come back to the sanctuary

195 (presbyterium) to the left side, and the archdeacon nods to the choir to sing, *O Lamb of God.*[122] And meantime whilst the breaking proceeds, the collets who hold the large bowls (scyphi) and cruets (amulae) respond, *O Lamb of God.* When the fraction is over the archdeacon takes the holy chalice from the subdeacon

200 and another deacon the paten from the collet and they go before the pontiff.

10. The Communion.

The pontiff takes the holy Elements (Sancta) from the paten,

---

[120] This appears to be a shortened form of the triple benediction of the Gallican Church.

[121] The sack was the badge of the collet at Rome, and was given to him at ordination. See line 171. On it were placed the consecrated Loaves (see line 189), the unconsecrated oblation-loaves being received by collets on linen cloths. See line 123.

[122] Walafrid Strabo, c. 22, says that the anthem Agnus Dei was introduced by Sergius at the fraction.

bites off a particle, with which he makes the sign of the cross over
the chalice, saying in an undertone, *May this commixture,* &c.
205 Then the pontiff partakes of the cup (confirmat) which is held by
the archdeacon. Then the bishops and presbyters receive the
holy Elements at the hand of the pontiff, and going to the left
[north] side of the altar, place their hands containing the holy
Elements upon the altar, and thus communicate. As soon as the
210 bishops and presbyters begin to communicate, the archdeacon
goes to the right side of the altar, and the collet stands before
him with the chief (prior) communion bowl, and he announces the
[next] station,[123] and all make answer, *Thanks be to God.* And then
he pours part [of the contents] of the chalice into the bowl. He
215 then hands the chalice to the bishop who communicated first, and
goes to the pontiff and receives the holy Element at his hand,
and the other deacons do likewise. And they go to the right side
of the altar and communicate. Then the chalice is administered
to them (confirmantur) by the same bishop who administered it
220 to the presbyters.

The pontiff then communicates the precentors and succentors.
Then the archdeacon takes the chalice back from the bishop, and
a subdeacon comes having a small strainer in his hand, who,
taking the holy Element out of the chalice, places it in the first of
225 the smaller bowls (fontes), out of which the archdeacon will
administer to the people, and the archdeacon empties the chalice
into the second chalice, and the collet pours part of [its contents]
into the first of the smaller bowls. Then the pontiff comes down
to communicate the people, and the archdeacon nods to the choir
230 to commence the communion anthem. And when the choir have
said it, subdeacons repeat it on the left side of the screen below
the throne. And when the chief people, tribunes, counts and
judges, and as many others as he chooses have been communicated

---

[123] In days of persecution this moment appears to have been chosen
to announce the next place of meeting because it was most likely to be
the moment when no non-Christians were present. Batiffol, p. 77.

[by the pontiff] he goes to the women's side below the screen, and
235 the deacons after him giving the cup (confirmantes) to the people.
Then when he gives word he returns to his seat, and priests
(sacerdotes) take up a position to communicate and give the cup
to the people below the sanctuary (presbyterium). Meanwhile the
pontiff sits in his seat, and a collet stands before him with the
240 holy paten, and subdeacons come before him, notaries and
district officials, and he communicates them, and the deacon
administers the cup to them.

Then the notaries take up a position before him with pen
and paper (? dhomum) in their hand, and whomever the pontiff
245 wishes to invite, he directs his name to be put down. And the
notaries come down from his seat and announce the invitations to
those whose names are down.

Meantime the priest comes and communicates the choir, and
the fourth in the choir holds the small bowl (fons) in his hand,
250 which was filled out of the first large bowl (scyphus), [124] and a
presbyter takes it from his hand and makes the sign of the cross
over it with the holy Element, and drops It into it—and let all
other presbyters do the same when they give the cup to the
people—and he gives the cup to the choir. And when the arch-
255 deacon sees that few remain to be communicated, he nods to the
choir to sing the *Gloria*. And the subdeacons take up *As it was
in the beginning*, and the choir repeat one verse.

---

[124] Four vessels are mentioned : 1, the small chalice (calix, line 223),
which appears to have been the one consecrated ; 2, the large chalice for
station days (calix stationarius, lines 113, 226), into which the people's
offerings of wine were poured as they were received ; 3, the large communion bowl (scyphus, lines 116, 139, 212, 249), in which the consecrated
wine was mixed with unconsecrated wine for the communion of the people;
there appear to have been more than one of these (lines 123, 171, 197) ;
4, the small communion bowls (fontes, lines 140, 171, 224, 249), into each
of which a portion of the holy Element was put before administration to
the people. The Westminster Inventory in Archæologia for 1890, p. 231,
mentions a Magnus calix cum duabus auriculis (handles) pro oblatis
deputatus.

11. THE CONCLUDING COLLECT.

Then the pontiff comes down from his seat and comes before
the altar and the tapers are placed behind him. Meantime the
260 priests and deacons wash their hands and give one another the kiss
in order and subdeacons mutually where they stand, likewise als)
the choir in the place where they stand. The collect (oratio)
having been said the deacon says, *Depart, mass is over,*[125] not he who
read the Gospel but some other one.

12. THE RECESSION.

265 Then the pontiff comes down from the altar and the deacons
with him and the subdeacons walk before him with the censer
which has been already mentioned and the tapers also go before
him carried by collets. And as he walks down the centre of the
sanctuary (presbyterium) the choir-subdeacon says, " Sir, command
270 a blessing !"[126] And the pontiff says the blessing-collect (oratio) and
they answer, *Amen.* When he comes out of the sanctuary (presbyterium), again the judges say, " Sir, command a blessing ! " And
when the blessing has been given they answer, *Amen.* And the
collets who carry the tapers before the pontiff stop outside the
275 door whilst the pontiff enters the sacristy and then put out the
lights.

[125] Florus of Lyons, De Act. Miss. gives this as the rendering of " Ite,
missa est." Amalarius, A.D. 829, De Eccles. Offic. iii. 36, gives another :
Missa is the singular legation of Christ to the Father on our account,
bearing about Him the marks of His passion. But in De Offic. Miss.
written at Rome, he says of these words : What do they mean but "Depart
to your houses. The legation to God on your account is complete, and
the prayers have been carried by angels to heaven."

[126] Le Brun observes that this is a polite way of saying Give a blessing,
just as we now say Command silence, for Be silent.

13.   The Unvesting.

The pontiff unvests and subdeacons take charge of his vestments and give them to the chamberlains.   The deacons unvest
outside the sacristy and collets take charge of their vestments.
280 And whilst the pontiff sits there, the chief hostilar (mansionarius
prior) of the church comes with a silver plate (bacea) with rolls
(pastilli), or, if there is no silver plate, with a dish (catinum), and
stands in front of the pontiff ; and the deacons come in order,
after them the precentor and succentor, likewise the controller of
285 the finances (vicedominus)[127] and the subdeacons, and they receive
rolls from the pontiff's hand,   Then wine is poured out (miscitur)
for the pontiff and the others aforesaid.   All being over, the
pontiff says a collect and they leave the sacristy.

[127] The οἰκόνομος whom every bishop was required by the Council
of Chalcedon, A.D. 451, to appoint to secure a witness to the honest
administration of the finances of the Church.   He afterwards developed
into the Vicar-general.

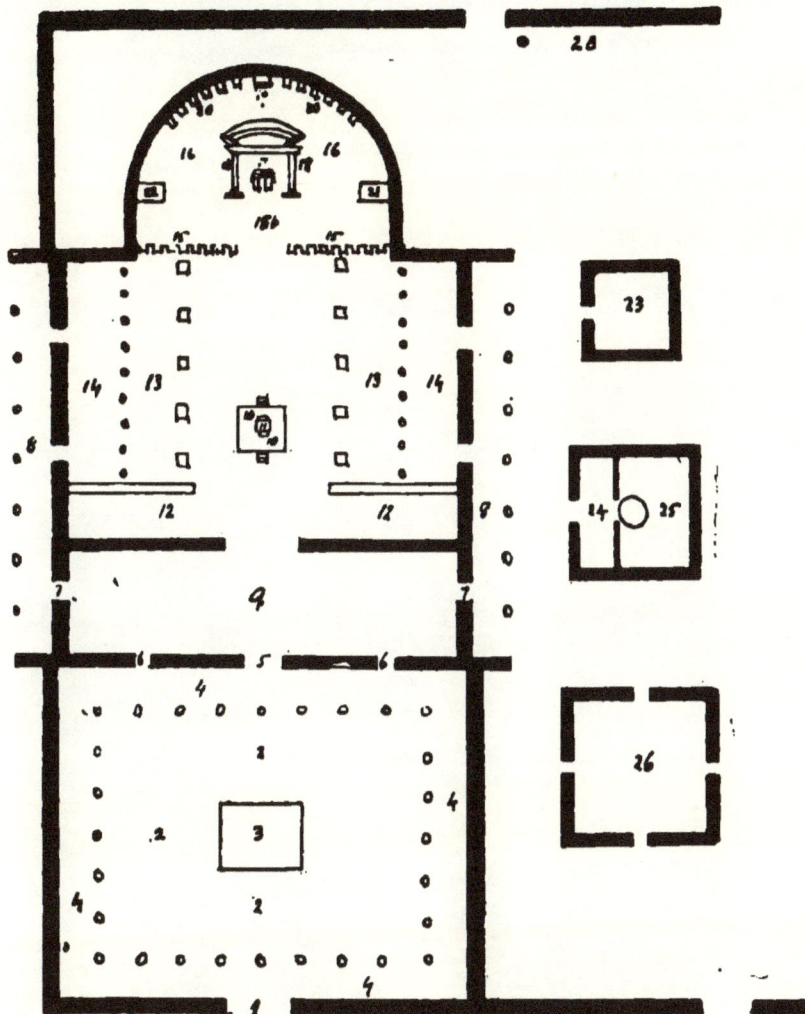

KEY TO THE ABOVE PLAN.

1.—*propylæum*, the great porch or first entrance into the area or court of the Church.
2.—The *atrium*, or court of the Church.
3.—*cantharus* or *phiala*, the water-fountain in the middle of the square.
4.—*exterior narthex*, or portico of " the weepers."

5.—The great or royal gate.
6.—The smaller gates.
7.—The northern and southern gates.
8.—The north and south cloisters.
9.—The *interior narthex*, or place of " catechumens " and " hearers."
10.—The singers' platform.
11.—The *ambo, pulpit*, or reading desk.
12.—The place of penitents.
13.—The places for men.
14.—The places for women, behind or above in galleries.

15.—The *cancelli*, or screen.
15b.—The *solium, bema*, or chancel.
16.—The *presbyterium*, or place of those in holy orders.
17.—The altar.
18.—The canopy over the altar.
19.—The bishop's seat.
20.—Seats for the presbyters.
21.—The *diaconicum minus*, or side table for the deacons' use.
22.—The *prothesis*, or table for the people's offerings.

23.—The *diaconicum majus*, or sacristy.
24.—The outer baptistry.
25.—The inner baptistry and font.
26.—*pastophoria*, dwelling-rooms, libraries, &c.
28.—*peribolos*, or place of sanctuary.

A History of the Somerset Carthusians. By
E. MARGARET THOMPSON.

> This Volume has 16 page Illustrations of Hinton Charter-House, Witham Friary, &c., by the Author's Sister, Miss L. B. THOMPSON, and will prove an interesting work to antiquarians, especially of Somersetshire and the West of England generally. Demy 8vo, 12s. *[Just ready.*

Cogitationes Concionales. Being 216 Short
Sermon Reflections on the Gospels for the Church's Year, founded upon Selected Readings from the "Summa Theologica" of S. THOMAS AQUINAS. By JOHN M. ASHLEY, B.C.L., Rector of Fewston; Author of "The Promptuary for Preachers," &c. Demy 8vo. 13 parts, 1s. each; 1 vol., cloth, 12s. *[Ready.*

Simpson's Life of Edmund Campion. This
valuable Book, having been out of print many years, has become very scarce, second-hand copies, when met with, realising fancy prices; it is now reprinted from a corrected copy, made by the learned Author before his death for a new edition. *[In the Press.*

The Great Commentary of à Lapide. The
Acts of the Apostles to Revelations, completing the New Testament. About 4 vols. *[In the Press.*

The Life of St. Jerome. By Fr. JOSEPHS of
Siquenza. Translated from the Spanish by MARIANA MONTEIRO, Author of "Basque Legends," "Life of Columbus," "History of Portugal," &c. *[Preparing.*

The Benedictine Calendar. By DOM. EGIDIUS
RANBECK, O.S.B. This remarkable work was first published in 1677, at the cost of the great Bavarian Monastery in Augsburg. The Life of a Benedictine Saint is given for every day in the year. The great merit of the work, however, consists in the beautiful Engravings, which illustrate the Lives. In the New Edition these Engravings have been most effectively reproduced. The accompanying Lives will be adaptations rather than translations of the originals, edited by a Father of the English Benedictine Congregation, and translated from the Latin by Professor MOHOLAN, M.A., of Downside College. 4 vols. *Vol. I. in the Press.* Also in 12 parts, 3s. 6d. each. *Part I. ready, Parts II. and III. in the Press.* Each part will contain One Month of the Calendar.

JOHN HODGES, BEDFORD STREET, STRAND, LONDON.

The Church of the Fathers, as seen in St. Osmond's Rite for the Cathedral of Salisbury. **A New and Revised Edition. 4 vols.** [*Preparing*.

Aurea Legenda: Alias Historia Lombardica: being a Collection of Lives of the Saints. By JACOBUS DE VORAGINE, Archbishop of Genoa. Translated and Edited by the Rev. S. J. EALES, D.C.L., Vicar of Stalisfield.
[*Preparing*.
This was one of the earliest works printed by William Caxton. He translated it into English by the command of William Earl of Arundel. His edition was printed at the Westminster Press in 1483.

The History and Fate of Sacrilege. By Sir HENRY SPELMAN, Kt. Edited, in part, from two MSS., Revised and Corrected. With a Continuation, large Additions, and an Introductory Essay. By Two Priests of the Church of England. Fourth Edition, with an Appendix bringing the work up to the present date, by C. F. S. WARREN, M.A. Demy 8vo, 12s. [*Just ready*.
₊ The Appendix may be had separately, price 1s.

Henry VIII. and the English Monasteries. An attempt to illustrate the History of their Suppression, with an Appendix and Maps, showing the situation of the religious houses at the time of their dissolution. By FRANCIS AIDAN GASQUET, D.D, O.S.B. 2 vols., 12s. each. Sixth Edition. May also be had in 2 vols., with Thirty-four page Illustrations and Five Maps, half-bound in Persian morocco, top edge gilt. Price 30s.; and in Twenty-two Parts at 1s. each. The Illustrations separately, price 5s.
[*On October 10th*.
BY THE SAME AUTHOR.

Edward VI. and the Book of Common Prayer. Its Origin illustrated by hitherto unpublished Documents. With Four Facsimile Pages of the MS. Third Thousand. Demy 8vo, 12s.

A Sketch of the Life and Mission of St. Benedict, with an Appendix containing a list of the Benedictine Churches and Monasteries in England with the date of their foundation. Third Thousand. 1s.

JOHN HODGES,
BEDFORD STREET, STRAND, LONDON.

www.ingramcontent.com/pod-product-compliance
Lightning Source LLC
Chambersburg PA
CBHW022041080426
42733CB00007B/935